Content

Hat and Scarf Set

A matching hat-and-muffler set is a winter-wardrobe must-have. For maximum impact, choose high-contrast colors for the stripes.

Designed by Josh Bennett

What you'll need:

YARN (4)

Any worsted-weight wool yarn that will give you the stated gauge.

3½oz/100g each in Dark Gray (A), Coral (B), Light Gray (C), Light Peach (D)

KNITTING NEEDLES

One pair each sizes 7 and 8 (4.5 and 5mm) needles or size to obtain gauge

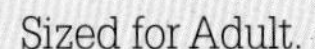

Sized for Adult.

Finished Measurements

Scarf Approximately 9" x 66" (23cm x 167.5cm)

Hat Head circumference (at ribbed brim) 17"/43cm

Length 10"/25.5cm

Gauges

- 18 sts and 24 rows to 4"/10cm over St st using larger needles.
- 20 sts and 26 rows to 4"/10cm over St st using smaller needles.

Take time to check your gauges.

K2, P2 Rib

(over a multiple of 4 sts)

Row 1 *K2, p2; rep from * to end.

Row 2 K the knit sts and p the purl sts.

Rep row 2 for k2, p2 rib.

Note: Cut colors not in use for more than 4 rows.

Scarf

With larger needles and A, cast on 40 sts and work 6 rows in k2, p2 rib. Change to St st (k on RS, p on WS) and work 8 rows.

Beg Stripes

Cont in St st as foll:

[2 rows B, 2 rows A] 3 times, 2 rows A, 30 rows B, [2 rows C, 2 rows D] 3 times, 2 rows C, 20 rows A, 2 rows D, 4 rows B, 40 rows C, 4 rows B, [2 rows D, 2 rows A] 3 times, [2 rows C, 2 rows A] 3 times, [2 rows B, 2 rows A] 3 times, 44 rows A, [2 rows A, 2 rows B] 3 times, [2 rows A, 2 rows C] 3 times, [2 rows A, 2 rows D] 3 times, 4 rows B, 40 rows C, 4 rows B, 2 rows D, 20 rows A, [2 rows C, 2 rows D] 3 times, 2 rows C, 30 rows B, 4 rows A, [2 rows B, 2 rows A] 3 times, 6 rows A.

Cont with A, work 6 rows in k2, p2 rib. Bind off.

Hat

With smaller needles and A, cast on 90 sts and work 6 rows in k2, p2 rib. Change to St st and work 4 rows.

Beg Stripes

Cont in St st and work in stripes as foll:

[2 rows C, 2 rows A] 3 times, 2 rows A, join B to complete hat, AT THE SAME TIME, when piece measures 7¼"/18.5cm from beg, end with WS row, shape crown.

Shape Crown

Row 1 (RS)*K7, k2tog; rep from* to end—80 sts.

Row 2 (and all WS rows) Purl.

Row 3 *K6, k2tog; rep from * to end—70 sts.

Row 5 *K5, k2tog; rep from * to end—60 sts.

Row 7 *K4, k2tog; rep from * to end—50 sts.

Row 9 *K3, k2tog; rep from * to end—40 sts.

Row 11 *K2, k2tog; rep from * to end—30 sts.

Row 13 *K1, k2tog; rep from * to end—20 sts.

Row 15 *K2tog; rep from * to end—10 sts.

Row 16 P10. Cut yarn, leaving 12"/30.5cm tail. Thread tapestry needle with tail and draw through rem sts. Sew seam. ■

PHOTOGRAPH BY PAUL AMATO

Fair Isle Scarf & Hat

New to two-color knitting? This easy set, in crisp navy and white, is the perfect beginner project.

Designed by Simona Merchant-Dest

What you'll need:

YARN (4)

Any worsted-weight superwash wool yarn that will give you the stated gauge.
16oz/450g in Navy (MC)
3½oz/100g in Natural (CC)

KNITTING NEEDLES

One pair size 8 (5mm) or size to obtain gauge
Size 8 (5mm) double-pointed needles (dpns) or size to obtain gauge

ADDITIONAL MATERIALS

Stitch holder
Tapestry needle

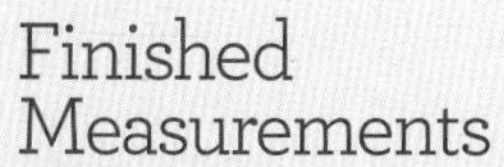

Finished Measurements

Scarf 9" x 87" (22.5cm x 217.5cm)
Hat circumference 22"/56cm

Gauge

Scarf 18 sts and 21 rows to 4"/10cm over St st using straight needles.
Hat 18 sts and 22 rows to 4"/10cm over St st in the round using dpns. Take time to check your gauge.

Note:
When changing colors, twist yarns on WS to prevent holes in work.

Scarf

SCARF FIRST HALF

With CC and straight needles, cast on 41 sts. Work in garter st for 8 rows, then work next 52 rows of scarf from text or scarf chart.

Rows 1–4 With MC, work in St st.
Row 5 (RS) With CC, *sl 1, k1; rep from * to last st, end sl 1.
Rows 6–8 Work in St st.
Row 9 With MC, *sl 1, k1; rep from * to last st, end sl 1.
Rows 10–12 Work in St st.
Row 13 With CC, *sl 1, k1; rep from * to last st, end sl 1.
Row 14 Purl.
Row 15 *K1 CC, k1 MC; rep from * to last st, end k1 CC.
Row 16 With MC, purl.
Rows 17–19 Work in St st.
Rows 20 and 26 *P1 CC, p2 MC; rep from * to last 2 sts, end p1 CC, p1 MC.
Rows 21 and 25 *K2 MC, k1 CC; rep from * to last 2 sts, end k2 MC.
Rows 22 and 24 P1 MC, *p1 CC, p2 MC; rep from * to last st, end p1 CC.
Row 23 With CC, knit.
Rep rows 1–26 once more.
With MC, work even in St st until piece measures 42"/106.5cm from beg, ending with a RS row. Place sts on holder.

SCARF SECOND HALF

Make as for Scarf First Half, ending with a WS row.

Finishing

With RS facing up, lay 2 scarf halves tog at holders. Graft together with Kitchener St or Three-Needle Bind-off.

Hat

BRIM

With CC and dpns, cast on 96 sts. Place marker and join for knitting in the round, taking care not to twist sts. Work in garter st for 9 rnds, then work next 23 rnds of hat from text or hat chart.

Rnds 1–4 With MC, knit.
Rnd 5 With CC, *sl 1, k1; rep from * to marker.
Rnds 6–8 Knit.
Rnd 9 With MC, *sl 1, k1; rep from * to marker.
Rnds 10–12 Knit.
Rnd 13 With CC, *sl 1, k1; rep from * to marker.
Rnd 14 Knit.
Rnd 15 *K1 CC, k1 MC; rep from * to marker.
Rnds 16–19 With MC, knit.
Rnd 20 *K1 CC, k2 MC; rep from * to marker.
Rnd 21 K1 MC, *k1 CC, k2 MC; rep from * to last st, end k1 MC.
Rnd 22 *K2 MC, k1 CC; rep from * to marker.
Rnd 23 With CC, knit. With MC, knit 2 rnds.

Crown shaping

Rnd 1 *K10, k2tog; rep from * to marker—88 sts.
Rnds 2–3 Knit.
Rnd 4 *K9, k2tog; rep from * to marker—80 sts.
Rnds 5–6 Knit.
Rnd 7 *K8, k2tog; rep from * to marker—72 sts.
Rnds 8–9 Knit.
Rnd 10 *K7, k2tog; rep from * to marker—64 sts.
Rnds 11, 13, 15, 17, and 19 Knit.
Rnd 12 *K6, k2tog; rep from * to marker—56 sts.
Rnd 14 *K5, k2tog; rep from * to marker—48 sts.
Rnd 16 *K4, k2tog; rep from * to marker—40 sts.
Rnd 18 *K3, k2tog; rep from * to marker—32 sts.
Rnd 20 *K2, k2tog; rep from * to marker—24 sts.
Rnd 21 *K1, k2tog; rep from * to marker—16 sts.
Rnd 22 *K2tog; rep from * to marker—8 sts.
Cut 12"/30.5cm tail, thread through rem sts and cinch tightly to close. ▪

(Charts on page 24)

PHOTOGRAPH BY JENNY ACHESON

Hoodie Scarf

What could be handier than an all-in-one hat and scarf? Pompoms on the scarf ends and hood ties are a fresh treat.

Designed by Linda Cyr

Finished Measurements

Scarf approx 5½" x 53" (14cm x 134.5cm)

Hood approx 10" x 12" (25.5cm x 30.5cm)

Gauge

20 sts and 24 rows to 4"/10cm over striped rib using size 8 (5mm) circular needle.

Take time to check your gauge.

Striped Rib 1

(multiple of 4 sts plus 3)

Row 1 (RS) With A, k2, *p2, k2; rep from *, end p1. Turn.

Row 2 (WS) Rep row 1. Do *not* turn. Slide sts to other end of needle.

Row 3 (WS) With B, k1, p2, *k2, p2; rep from * to end. Turn.

Row 4 (RS) Rep row 3. Do *not* turn. Slide sts to other end of needle.

Rep rows 1–4 for striped rib 1.

Striped Rib 2 (multiple of 4 sts plus 1)

Row 1 (RS) With A, *k2, p2; rep from *, end k1. Turn.

Row 2 (WS) With A, *p2, k2; rep from *, end p1. Do *not* turn. Slide sts to other end of needle.

Row 3 (WS) With B, p1, *k2, p2; rep from * to end. Turn.

Row 4 (RS) With B, k1, *p2, k2; rep from * to end. Do *not* turn. Slide sts to other end of needle.

Rep rows 1–4 for striped rib II.

Scarf (make 2)

With A, cast on 27 sts. Work in striped rib 1 until piece measures 26½"/67.5cm from beg, end with row 4. Bind off.

What you'll need:

YARN (4)

Any worsted-weight wool or wool-blend yarn that will give you the stated gauge.

3½oz/100g each in Light Blue (A) and Cream (B)

1oz/30g in Mint Green (C)

KNITTING NEEDLES

Size 8 (5mm) circular needle, 24"/60cm long or size to obtain gauge

Size J-10 (6mm) crochet hook

ADDITIONAL MATERIALS

Stitch holders, stitch markers and safety pin

Hood

Sew bound-off edges of scarf tog forming center back seam. Along one long edge of scarf, place markers 9"/23 from each side of center back seam. With RS facing and A, pick up and k 42 sts evenly spaced from first marker to seam, 1 st in seam, then 42 sts from seam to 2nd marker—85 sts. Beg with row 2, work in stripe pat 2 for 47 rows.

Shape Right Side of Hood

Next (Dec) Row Work in rib across first 26 sts, k2tog, place next 29 sts on holder for center of hood and rem 28 sts onto separate holder for left side of hood. Turn. Cont on right side of hood as foll:

Next Row Work even.

Next (Dec) Row Work in rib to last 2 sts, k2tog—26 sts. Rep last 2 rows 3 times more—23 sts.

Next (Dec) Row P2tog, work in rib to end—22 sts.

Next (Dec) Row Work in rib to last 2 sts, k2tog—21 sts. Rep last 2 rows twice more—17 sts.

Last (Dec) Row P2tog, work in rib to end. Bind off rem 16 sts.

Center of Hood

Place 29 sts center hood back on needle. Cont in rib as established for 48 rows. Bind off.

Shape Left Side of Hood

Place left side of hood sts back on needle.

Next (Dec) Row K2tog, work in rib to end—27 sts. Cont to work as for right side of hood, reversing shaping.

Finishing

Sew hood seams.

Drawstring Casing

With RS facing and C, pick up and k 109 sts evenly spaced across front edge of hood. Beg with a k row, work in rev St st for 7 rows. Bind off. Fold casing in half to WS and sew edge in place.

Drawstring

With crochet hook and 2 strands of B held tog, ch for 40"/101.5cm. Fasten off. Fasten safety pin to one end of ch. Insert safety pin between sts along front edge of casing, 2½"/6.5cm from bottom edge of hood. Thread drawstring through casing, exiting safety pin 2½"/6.5cm from opposite bottom edge.

Pompoms (make 12 pieces)

With C, make 10 pompoms 1½"/4cm in diameter. Sew 5 pompoms evenly spaced along each end of scarf. With B, make 2 pompoms 2½"/6.5cm in diameter. Sew one to each end of drawstring. ▪

PHOTOGRAPH BY JENNY ACHESON

Bow-Tie Necklet

This pretty garter-stitch scarf has bow-shaped ends that tuck through a ribbed tube.

Designed by Julie Hines

Finished Measurements

Approx 5" x 30" (12.5cm x 76cm)

Gauge

24 sts and 38 rows to 4"/10cm over garter st using size 6 (4mm) needles. Take time to check your gauge.

K1, P1 Rib

(over an odd number of sts)

Row 1 *K1, p1; rep from * to last st, k1.
Row 2 K the knit sts, and p the purl sts.
Rep row 2 for k1, p1 rib.

Stitch Glossary

Kf-b Inc 1 st by knitting into the front and back of next st.

What you'll need:

YARN (3)
Any DK-weight wool-blend yarn that will give you the stated gauge.
3½oz/100g in Beige

KNITTING NEEDLES
One pair size 6 (4mm) needles or size to obtain gauge
Three size 6 (4mm) double-pointed needles (dpns)

Bow Tie

With size 6 (4mm) single-pointed needles, cast on 3 sts.
Inc Row Kf-b, k to end.
Rep Inc Row until there are 30 sts on needle.
Work even in garter st (k every row) until piece measures 4½"/11.5cm from beg.

Divide for Keyhole
Next Row *Sl 1 st to first dpn, sl next st to 2nd dpn; rep from * until sts are divided equally on 2 dpns.
Next Row With 3rd dpn, work the 15 sts of front dpn in k1, p1 rib for 2"/5cm, end with an inside row.
Cut yarn. 2nd (unworked) dpn is at front. Re-join yarn to 2nd dpn.
Work same as for first dpn, end with an outside row.
Turn work so that working yarn is at back of work.

Complete Keyhole
Next Row With single-pointed needle, *k1 from front dpn, k1 from back dpn; rep from * until all 30 sts are on one single-pointed needle.
Work in garter st until piece measures 23½"/59.5cm. Work 2nd keyhole same as first. Once all 30 sts have been knitted onto one single-pointed needle, work even in garter st for 3"/7.5cm.
Dec Row K1, ssk, k to end.
Rep Dec Row until 3 sts rem.
Next Row K3tog. Fasten off. To wear as shown, pull one end of bow tie through opposite keyhole. ▪

PHOTOGRAPH BY ROSE CALLAHAN

Ridged Cowl

Ridges add a classic touch to this on-trend accessory.

Designed by Faith Hale

What you'll need:

YARN (3)
Any DK-weight wool/silk-blend yarn that will give you the stated gauge.
1¾oz/50g in Natural

KNITTING NEEDLES
One size 5 (3.75mm) circular needle, 24"/60cm long or size to obtain gauge

ADDITIONAL MATERIALS
Stitch marker

Finished Measurements

Circumference 26"/66cm
Height 9"/23cm

Gauge

22 sts and 45 rnds to 4"/10cm over ridge pat.
Take time to check your gauge.

Note:
This piece is reversible as the ridge pat looks good on either side.

Ridge Pattern

Purl 6 rnds, knit 3 rnds.
Rep these 9 rnds for ridge pat.

Cowl

Cast on 146 sts. Taking care not to twist sts, place marker and join for knitting in the round.
Work in ridge pat for 11 reps. Purl 3 more rnds. Bind off loosely purlwise. ■

PHOTOGRAPH BY ROSE CALLAHAN

Bamboo Scarf

Short on time? Go big-impact with this easy textured-rib neck wrap.

Designed by Tanis Gray

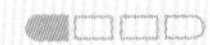

What you'll need:

YARN (5)
Any bulky-weight acrylic /wool-blend yarn that will give you the stated gauge.
7oz/200g in Pink

KNITTING NEEDLES
One pair size 10½ (6.5mm) or size to obtain gauge

Finished Measurements

60" x 5¼" (152.5cm x 13.5cm)

Gauge

18 sts and 16 rows (unstretched) to 4"/10cm over Bamboo Stitch.
Take time to check your gauge.

Bamboo Stitch

Rows 1, 3, 7, and 9 (RS) *P2, k4; rep from * to end.
Rows 2, 4, 8, and 10 (WS) *P4, k2; rep from * to end.
Row 5 *P8, k4; rep from * to end.
Row 6 *P4, k8; rep from * to end.
Row 11 P2, *k4, p8; rep from *, end last rep p6.
Row 12 K6, * p4, k8; rep from *, end last rep k2.
Rep rows 1–12 for Bamboo Stitch.

Scarf

Cast on 24 sts. Work in Bamboo Stitch until piece measures 60"/152.5cm. Bind off. ▪

PHOTOGRAPH BY JENNY ACHESON

Cabled Shawl

Oatmeal goes uptown in this elegant wrap knit in reverse stockinette stitch with easy cables and a crocheted picot border.

Designed by Tanis Gray

Finished Measurements
19" x 56" (48.5cm x 142cm)

Gauges
- 13 sts and 20 rows to 4"/10cm over St st using size 9 (5.5mm) needle.
- 18-st cable panel = 3¼"/8cm at row 21 using size 9 (5.5mm) needle.

Take time to check your gauges.

Stitch Glossary
8-st LPC Sl 3 sts to cn and hold to *front*, k3, p2; k3 from cn.

Shawl
Cast on 75 sts.

Row 1 (RS) P5, work row 1 of Cable Panel Chart over next 18 sts, p29, work row 1 of Cable Panel Chart over next 18 sts, p5.

Row 2 (WS) K5, work row 2 of Cable Panel Chart over next 18 sts, k29, work row 2 of Cable Panel Chart over next 18 sts, k5.

Cont in this way through row 28 of Cable Panel Chart, then rep rows 1–28 eight times more, then rows 1–22 once more.

Bind off loosely in pat.

Finishing
Edging

With RS facing and crochet hook, work sc evenly around edges of shawl for 2 rnds.

Next rnd Ch 1, sc 1 in next sc, *ch 5, work sl st in ch, skip 1 sc, sc in next 5 sc; rep from * around. Fasten off.

Lightly block. ▪

What you'll need:

YARN (5)

Any bulky-weight wool-blend yarn that will give you the stated gauge.

16oz/450g in Natural Tweed

KNITTING NEEDLES

One size 9 (5.5mm) circular needle, 24"/60cm long or size to obtain gauge

One size 1-9 (5.5mm) crochet hook

ADDITIONAL MATERIALS

Cable needle (cn)

CABLE PANEL

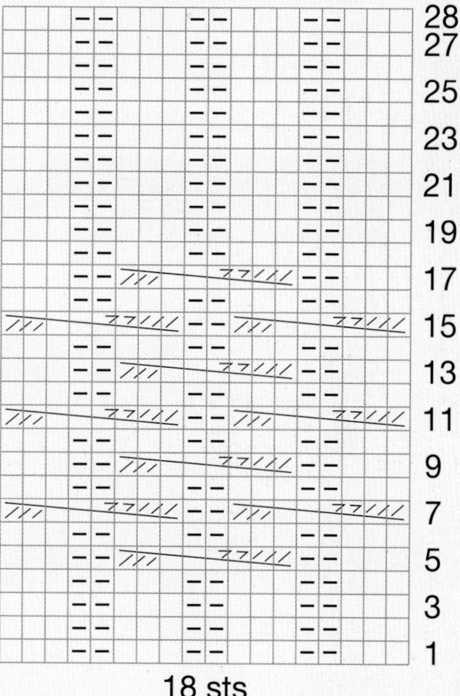

STITCH KEY

- ☐ K on RS, p on WS
- ⊟ P on RS, k on WS
- 8-st LPC

PHOTOGRAPH BY ROSE CALLAHAN

PHOTOGRAPH BY ROSE CALLAHAN

Trinity Stitch Scarf

Metallic accents add drama to eveningwear.

Designed by Julie Gaddy

What you'll need:

YARN (3)

Any DK-weight rayon/metallic-blend yarn that will give you the stated gauge.
3½oz/100g each in Silver (MC) and Silver/Black multi (CC)

KNITTING NEEDLES

One pair size 8 (5mm) needles or size to obtain gauge

Finished Measurements

Approximately 6½" x 60" (16.5cm x 152.5cm)

Gauge

30 sts and 26 rows to 4"/10cm over trinity stitch using size 8 (5mm) needles.
Take time to check your gauge.

Trinity Stitch

(over a multiple of 4 sts)

Set-up row (WS) Sl1, k1, *[k1, p1, k1] into next st, p3tog; rep from * to last 2 sts, k2.

Row 1 (RS) Sl 1, k1, purl across row to last 2 sts, k2.

Row 2 Sl 1, k1, *p3tog, [k1, p1, k1] into next st; rep from * to last 2 sts, k2.

Row 3 Sl 1, k1, p to last 2 sts, k2.

Row 4 Sl 1, k1, *[k1, p1, k1] into next st, p3tog; rep from * to last 2 sts, k2.

Notes:

1. Slip first st of every row with yarn in front as if to purl. Move yarn to back of work, between needles, before knitting the 2nd st.
2. On color change rows, sl 1, then pick up new color from under old color after the old color has been moved to the back of work.
3. Add new ball of yarn by knitting a few sts with both the old ball and the new. This keeps the edge of the scarf uniform.

Scarf

With MC, cast on 52 sts. Work set-up row and row 1 of trinity st pat.
*Change to CC and work rows 2 and 3.
Change to MC and work rows 4 and 1.
Rep from * until scarf measures approx 60"/152.5cm from beg, end with a row 1.
With MC, work row 2. Bind off knitwise. ▪

Lace Wrap

Soft and airy, this shawl is the ultimate summer coverup.

Designed by Cecily Glowik

PHOTOGRAPH BY ROSE CALLAHAN

What you'll need:

YARN (1)

Any super-fine, lace-weight bamboo yarn that will give you the stated gauge.

5½oz/150g in Lilac

KNITTING NEEDLES

Size 10 (6mm) needles or size to obtain gauge

Finished Measurements

14" x 60" (35.5cm x 152.5cm)

Gauge

19 sts and 21 rows to 4"/10cm over lace pat, after blocking.

Take time to check your gauge.

Lace Pattern (multiple of 9 sts plus 4)

Rows 1 and 3 (WS) Purl.

Row 2 K3, *yo, k2, ssk, k2tog, k2, yo, k1; rep from * to last st, end k1.

Row 4 K2, *yo, k2, ssk, k2tog, k2, yo, k1; rep from * to last st, end k2.

Rep rows 1–4 for lace pat.

Shawl

Cast on 67 sts. Work in lace pat until piece measures 58"/147.5cm, ending with a WS row. Bind off.

Finishing

Block piece to 14" x 60"/35.5cm x 152.5cm. ■

Ridged Bag

Bands of garter stitching give the stockinette strips of this tote their touchable rippled effect.

Designed by Faith Hale

Finished Measurements

Approx 12" wide x 9" tall (30.5cm x 23cm)

Gauges

- 18 sts and 24 rnds to 4"/10cm over St st using size 7 (4.5mm) needles.
- 18 sts and 40 rnds to 4"/10cm over garter st using size 7 (4.5mm) needles.

Take time to check your gauges.

Garter St

(in rows)

Knit every row.

Garter St

(in rounds)

Purl 1 rnd, knit 1 rnd.

Rep these 2 rnds for garter st in rnds.

What you'll need:

YARN

Any worsted-weight wool solid and variegated yarns that will give you the stated gauge.
3½oz/100g each in Navy (MC) and Blue Variegated (CC)

KNITTING NEEDLES

One size 7 (4.5mm) circular needle, 20"/50cm long or size to obtain gauge

ADDITIONAL MATERIALS

Two bag handles
Stitch marker

Sides

With MC, cast on 100 sts. Place marker and join for knitting in the round.

**Beg with a purl rnd, work garter st in rnds for 7 rnds. Change to CC.

Next rnd Knit into front and back (kfb) of each st around—200 sts. Knit 9 rnds.

Next rnd *K2tog; rep from * around—100 sts. Change to MC.**

Rep from ** to ** 3 times more.

With MC, work garter st in rnds for 7 rnds. Bind off knitwise.

Bottom

With MC, cast on 13 sts. Work garter st in rows until piece measures approx 10½"/26.5cm, or until piece fits along cast-on edge of bag. Bind off knitwise.

Finishing

With MC, sew bottom to sides of bag along cast-on edge. Using photo for reference and MC, sew handles to top of bag. ▪

PHOTOGRAPH BY PAUL AMATO

Banded Mittens

This basic mitten pattern can be sized for the entire family.

Designed by Linda Cyr

PHOTOGRAPH BY MARCUS TULLIS

What you'll need:

YARN (4)
Any worsted-weight wool-blend yarn that will give you the stated gauge.
1¾oz/50g each in Light Blue (A) and Sage Green (B)

KNITTING NEEDLES
One set (5) size 7 (4.5mm) dpns or size to obtain gauge

ADDITIONAL MATERIALS
Stitch markers
Scrap yarn

Sizes

Sized for Child (Woman, Man).

Finished Measurements

Palm 6½ (7¼, 9)"/16.5 (18.5, 23)cm
Length 6 (8¾, 10¾)"/15.5 (22, 27.5)cm

Gauge

20 sts and 28 rnds to 4"/10cm over St st using size 7.5 (4.5mm) needles.
Take time to check your gauge.

Stripe Pattern

2 rnds B, 2 rnds A, 19 rnds B, 2 rnds A, 2 rnds B, then cont with A to end of piece.

Mitten

With A, cast on 32 (36, 44) sts.
Divide sts evenly over 4 dpns, place marker (pm) and join for knitting in the round. Work in k2, p2 rib for 1¾ (2¼, 2¾)"/4.5 (5.5, 7)cm.
Next Rnd K15 (17, 21), pm, k2, pm work to end of rnd. Knit 3 (4, 4) rnds.
Inc Rnd K to marker, sl marker, M1, k to next marker M1, sl marker, k to end—34 (38, 46) sts. K 1 (1, 2) rnds.
Rep last 2 (2, 3) rnds 3 (4, 4) times more—40 (46, 54) sts, AT THE SAME TIME, when 9 (12, 15) rnds of St st have been worked above rib, work first 4 rnds of Stripe Pat. After all incs have been worked, and ending with 2 rows A, cont in St st and Stripe pat and work as foll:

Thumb Gusset

Next Rnd With B, k14 (16, 20), sl next 12 (14, 14) sts to scrap yarn for thumb, cast on 4 sts, k to end of rnd.
Cont in pat on 32 (36, 44) sts until hand measures 1½ (2¼ 3)"/4 (5.5, 7.5)cm from thumb opening, or 1 (2, 2¼)"/2.5 (5, 5.5)cm shorter than desired length of mitten.

Top Shaping

Dec Rnd [K1, ssk, k11 (13, 17), pm, k2tog] twice—28 (32, 40) sts.
Knit 1 (4, 3) rnds.
Dec Rnd [K1, ssk, k to marker, sl marker, k2tog] twice—24 (28, 36) sts.
Knit 1 (4, 3) rnds.
Rep Dec Rnd every other rnd 0 (0, 2) times more, then every rnd 4 times—8 (12, 12) sts.
Bind off and sew rem sts tog, or place sts evenly on 2 dpns and use Kitchener st to graft sts tog.

Thumb

Sl sts from scrap yarn to dpns, rejoin yarn to inside of thumb, pick up and k 4 sts along cast-on sts, pm for beg of rnd—16 (18, 18) sts.
Work in St st and B until thumb measures 1½ (2, 2½)"/4 (5, 6.5)cm.
Dec Rnd [K2, k2tog] 4 times, k 0 (2, 2)—12 (14, 14) sts. Knit 1 rnd.
Dec Rnd K2tog around. Cut yarn leaving an 8"/20.5cm tail, thread through rem 6 (7, 7) sts and cinch tightly to close. ▪

Lace Rib Hat

Pretty eyelets form the fabric of this feminine hat.

Designed by Kathy North

PHOTOGRAPH BY MARCUS TULLIS

What you'll need:

YARN (4)
Any worsted-weight wool-blend yarn that will give you the stated gauge.
3½oz/100g in Natural

KNITTING NEEDLES
One size 8 (5mm) circular needle, 16"/40cm long, or size to obtain gauge
One set (5) size 8 (5mm) double-pointed needles (dpns)
Stitch marker

Sizes

Sized for Small, Medium, Large and shown in size Large.

Finished Measurements

Circumference 18 (20, 22)"/45.5 (51, 56)cm

Gauges

- 20 sts and 26 rows to 4"/10cm over St st using size 8 (5mm) needles.
- 1 pattern rep to 1½"/4cm using size 8 (5mm) needles.

Take time to check your gauges.

Twisted Rib

Rnd 1 *K1 tbl, p1; rep from * around.
Rep Rnd 1 for Twisted Rib.

Hat

With circular needle, cast on 84 (92, 106) sts. Place marker and join, taking care not to twist sts. Work in Twisted Rib for 8 rnds, dec 0 (1, 1) st at end of last rnd—84 (91, 105) sts.
Change to Lace Pat as foll:
Rnds 1 and 2 *K5, p2; rep from * around.
Rnd 3 *K2tog, yo, k1, yo, ssk, p2; rep from * around.
Rnd 4 *K5, p2; rep from * around. Rep Rnds 1–4 until piece measures 6¾ (7, 7½)"/17 (18, 19)cm from beg, ending with a row 4.

Shape Crown

Shape crown as foll, changing to dpns when sts no longer fit comfortably on circular needle:
Next Rnd *K5, p2tog; rep from * around—72 (78, 90) sts.
Next Rnd *K2tog, k1, k2tog, p1; rep from * around—48 (52, 60) sts.
Next Rnd *K2tog; rep from * around—24 (26, 30) sts.
Next Rnd *K2tog; rep from * around—12 (13, 15) sts. Cut yarn, leaving a 6"/15cm tail. Thread through rem sts and cinch tightly to close. ■

Drawstring Backpack

Why send her to school with a store-bought rucksack when a hand-knit one is such a snap to make?

Designed by Jenn Jarvis

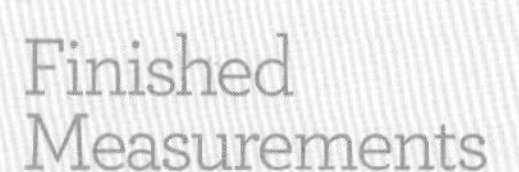

Finished Measurements

Circumference 24"/61cm
Height 14"/35.5cm

Gauge

18 sts and 24 rnds to 4"/10cm over St st in the round using size 7 (4.5,mm) needles.
Take time to check your gauge.

Bag

With A, cast on 108 sts for lower edge of bag. Place marker (of contrasting color) and join for knitting in the round taking care not to twist sts on needle.
Next Rnd K27 sts, pm, k54, pm, k to end of rnd marker. Knit 2 rnds.
Next Rnd [K to 6 sts before marker, k2tog, yo, k4, sl m, k4, yo, k2tog] twice, k to end of rnd marker.
Cont in St st until piece measures 13"/33cm from beg.
Eyelet Rnd K4, yo, k2tog, [k7, yo, k2tog] 11 times, k3.
Work until piece measures 14"/35.5cm from beg. Bind off purlwise.

Bottom

Pick up and knit 108 sts along cast-on row. Place marker and join.
Purl 1 rnd. Knit 2 rnds.
Next Rnd *K7, k2tog; rep from * around—96 sts. K 3 rnds.
Next Rnd *K6, k2tog; rep from * around—84 sts. K 3 rnds.
Next Rnd *K5, k2tog; rep from * around—72 sts. K 1 rnd.
Next Rnd *K4, k2tog; rep from * around—60 sts. K 1 rnd.
Next Rnd *K3, k2tog; rep from * around—48 sts. K 1 rnd.
Next Rnd *K2, k2tog; rep from * around—36 sts. **Rnd** 1 rnd.
Next rnd *K1, k2tog; rep from * around—24 sts. K 1 rnd.
Next Rnd *K2tog; rep from * around—12 sts.
Next Rnd *K2tog; rep from * around—6 sts.
Cut yarn and thread through rem sts. Cinch tightly to close.

What you'll need:

YARN
Any worsted-weight
superwash wool yarn
that will give you the stated gauge.
7oz/200g in Teal (A)
1¾oz/50g each in Light Orange (B)
and Red Multi (C)

KNITTING NEEDLES
One size 7 (4.5mm) circular needle, 24"/60cm long
One set (5) size 7 (4.5mm) dpns
One size H-8 (5mm) crochet hook

ADDITIONAL MATERIALS
Stitch markers (one in contrasting color)
1 yd/1m lining fabric
1 sheet Timtex
Sewing needle and thread
Sewing machine (optional)

I-cord Straps

Work two 120"/305cm I-cord straps as foll:
With C, cast on 4 sts.
***Row 1 (RS)** K4. Do *not* turn. Slide sts to beg of needle to work next row from RS.
Rep from * for I-cord. Thread cord through top of bag and thread both ends through bottom eyelets and knot together.

Flower

Layer 1 With B and crochet hook, ch 6. In the 6th ch from hook, work [dc, ch 2] 7 times.
Join with sl st in 3rd ch st of initial chain (8 spokes in wheel).
Next Rnd Ch 1, work [sc, ch 1, 2 dc, ch 1, sc] over each ch-2 arch. Join with sl st to first sc. Fasten off.
Layer 2 With C, make a slip knot on hook. With WS facing, insert hook under a center spoke and work sl st to join yarn, ch 6, work [dc, ch 3] around each remaining spoke, sl st in 3rd ch of ch-6 (8 spokes in C).
Next rnd Ch 1, turn to RS with Layer 1 on top, work [sc, ch 1, 3 dc, ch 1, sc] over each ch-3 arch, join in first sc. Fasten off.
Layer 3 With B, make a slip knot on hook. With WS facing, insert hook under a Layer 2 spoke and work sl st to join yarn, ch 7, work [dc, ch 4] around each remaining spoke, sl st in 3rd ch of ch-6 (8 spokes in B).
Next rnd Ch 1, turn to RS with Layer 1 on top, work [sc, ch 1, 4 dc, ch 1, sc] over each ch-4 arch, join in first sc. Fasten off.
Layer 4 With C, make a slip knot on hook. With WS facing, insert hook under a Layer 3 spoke and work sl st to join yarn, ch 8, work [dc, ch 5] around each remaining spoke, sl st in 3rd ch of ch-6 (8 spokes in B).
Next Rnd Ch 1, turn to RS with Layer 1 on top, work [sc, ch 1, 5 dc, ch 1, sc] over each ch-5 arch, join in first sc. Fasten off.
Layer 5 With B, make a slip knot on hook. With WS facing, insert hook under a Layer 4 spoke and work sl st to join yarn, ch 9, work [dc, ch 6] around each remaining spoke, sl st in 3rd ch of ch-6 (8 spokes in B).
Next Rnd Ch 1, turn to RS with Layer 1 on top, work [sc, ch 1, 6 dc, ch 1, sc] over each ch-6 arch, join in first sc. Fasten off.
Sew to front of bag.

Lining

Cut Timtex in a circle to fit in bottom of bag. Place in bottom of bag.
Using bag for reference, cut fabric to fit bottom circle and a piece to cover side of bag. Sew side piece to bottom piece, sew up side seam. Press a ¼"/.5cm hem at top of side piece, hand sew into bag. ■

PHOTOGRAPH BY ROSE CALLAHAN

Striped Beach Bag

This fun-in-the-sun tote, lined for stability, carries sunscreen, snacks and paperbacks in style.

Designed by Tanis Gray

Finished Measurements

18½" wide x 16" tall (47cm x 40.5cm)

Gauge

16 sts and 29 rows to 4"/10cm over St st using size 5 (3.75mm) needles. Take time to check your gauge.

What you'll need:

YARN (4)
Any worsted-weight cotton yarn that will give you the stated gauge.
1¾oz/50g each in Turquoise (A), Medium Blue (B), Red (C), Bright Pink (D), Yellow (E), Olive Green (F), Pale Green (G) and White (H)

KNITTING NEEDLES
One pair size 5 (3.75mm) needles or size to obtain gauge
One pair size F-5 (3.75mm) crochet hook

ADDITIONAL MATERIALS
1 yd/1m cotton fabric
1 yd/1m thick interfacing
Tapestry needle
Sewing needle and matching thread
Iron
Scissors

Bag Side (make 2)

With A, cast on 60 sts. Work in St st for 10 rows.

Row 11 (RS) Change to H, k1, M1, k to last st, M1, k1—62 sts.
Row 12 Knit.
Rows 13–22 Change to B, work in St st.
Row 23 Rep row 11—64 sts.
Row 24 Knit.
Rows 25–34 Change to C, work in St st.
Row 35 Rep row 11—66 sts.
Row 36 Knit.
Rows 37–46 Change to D, work in St st.
Row 47 Rep row 11—68 sts.
Row 48 Knit.
Rows 49–58 Change to E, work in St st.
Row 59 Rep row 11—70 sts.
Row 60 Knit.
Rows 61–70 Change to F, work in St st.
Row 71 Rep row 11—72 sts.
Row 72 Knit.
Rows 73–82 Change to G, work in St st.
Row 83 Rep row 11—74 sts.
Row 84 Knit.
Rows 85–94 Change to A, work in St st.
Row 95 K25, join a 2nd ball of yarn, bind off 24, knit to end to separate for handle.
Rows 96–98 Work both sides at the same time in St st.
Row 99 Change to H, right side k1, M1, knit to end; left side k to last st, M1, k1—26 sts each side.
Row 100 Knit.
Rows 101–102 Change to B, work in St st.
Row 103 K26, cast on 24 sts, k to end to join for handle—76 sts.
Rows 104–110 Work in St st.
Row 111 Change to H, [k2tog] twice, k to last 4 sts, [k2tog] twice—72 sts.
Row 112 [P2tog] twice, p to last 4 sts, [p2tog] twice—68 sts.
Rows 113 and 115 Change to C, rep row 111—64 sts.
Rows 114 and 116 Rep row 112—52 sts.
Row 117 Bind off 15 sts, k to end—37 sts.
Row 118 Bind off 15 sts, [p2tog] twice, p to last 4 sts, [p2tog] twice—18 sts.
Rows 119–121 Work in St st.
Bind off.

Bag Bottom

With A, cast on 15 sts. Work in St st for 4 rows.

Next Row (RS) K1, M1, k to last st, M1, k1—17 sts. Purl one row. Rep last 2 rows 5 times more—27 sts. Work even in St st for 5"/12.5cm.
Next Row (RS) K2tog, k to last 2 sts, k2tog—25 sts. Purl one row. Rep last 2 rows 5 times more—15 sts. Bind off.

Lining

Trace and cut 2 pieces of interfacing to shape of bag sides and 1 oval bottom. Cut pieces of cotton fabric to match interfacing pieces, plus ½"/1.5cm for selvage. Sew fabric pieces to corresponding pieces of interfacing. Iron flat. Cut out handle and secure fabric edges to interfacing. Sew sides of lining for main body of bag together (RS facing each other so fabric lining is inside). Sew oval to bottom edges of bag lining.

Finishing

With H and crochet hook, crochet sides of knitted bag together. Fit knitted bag around fabric-covered interfacing.
With H and crochet hook, crochet bottom of knitted bag to sides. Work one row of sc around top of bag and edges of handles. Secure handle and top of bag by hand-basting interfacing to knitted pieces. ▪

PHOTOGRAPH BY ROSE CALLAHAN

 (continued from page 4)

For a softer look, flip your A and B colors.

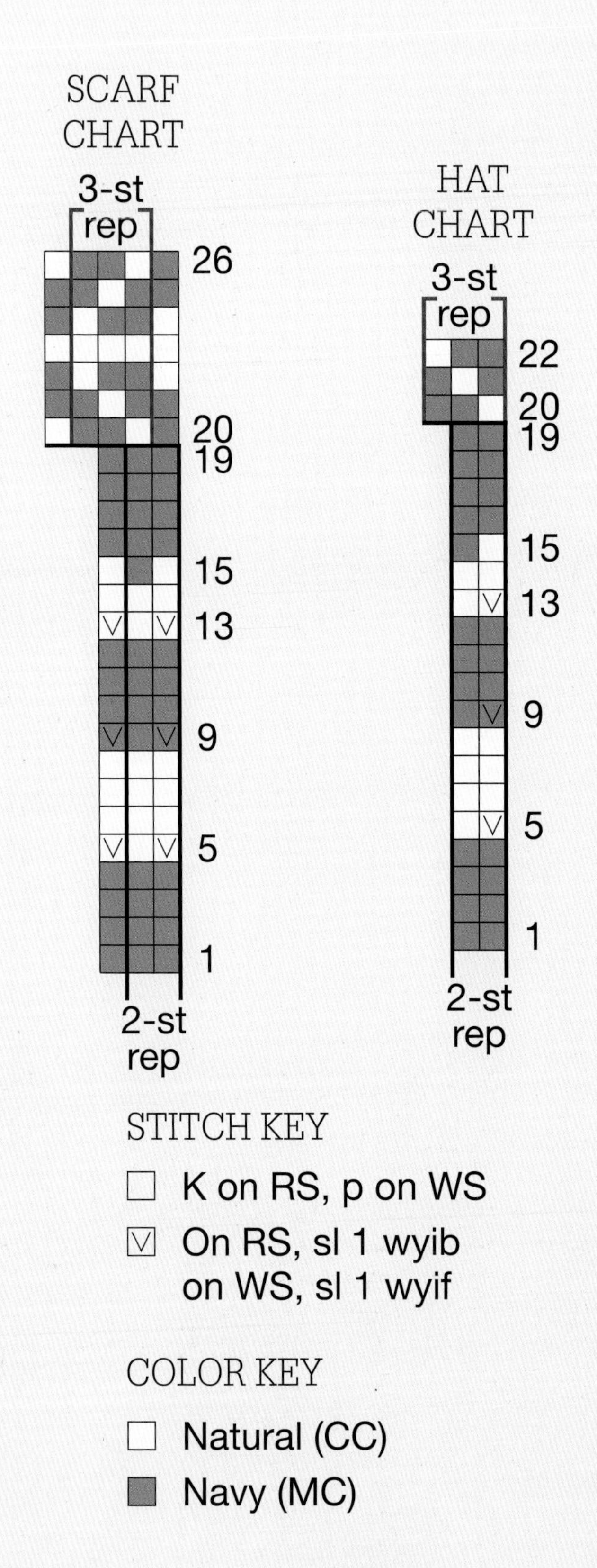